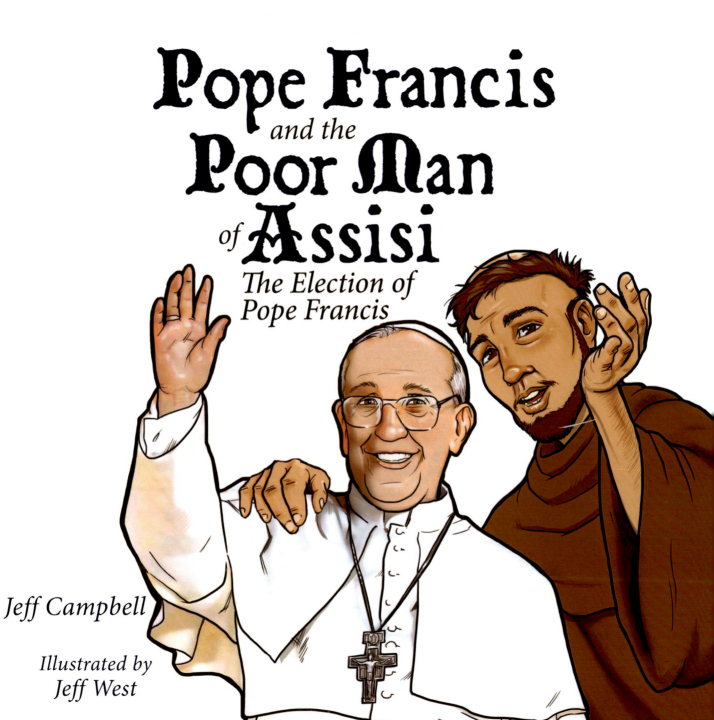

Pope Francis
and the
Poor Man
of Assisi
The Election of Pope Francis

Jeff Campbell

Illustrated by
Jeff West

Pope Francis and the Poor Man of Assisi
The Election of Pope Francis
Jeffrey Campbell

Illustrated by Jeff West

Illustration, cover and book design: Tau Publishing Design Department

For information regarding permission, write to:
Tau Publishing, LLC
Attention: Permissions Dept.
4727 North 12th Street
Phoenix, AZ 85014

ISBN 978-1-61956-251-6

First Edition September 2014
10 9 8 7 6 5 4 3 2 1

Published and printed in the United States of America by Tau Publishing, LLC, an imprint of Vesuvius Press, Incorporated
For additional inspirational books visit us at TauPublishing.com

TauPublishing.com

Words of Inspiration

Dedication

For all those who take to heart these words from Matthew 25:35-40

For I was hungry and you gave me food, I was thirsty and you gave me drink, a stranger and you welcomed me,

naked and you clothed me, ill and you cared for me, in prison and you visited me.'

Then the righteous* will answer him and say, 'Lord, when did we see you hungry and feed you, or thirsty and give you drink?

When did we see you a stranger and welcome you, or naked and clothe you?

When did we see you ill or in prison, and visit you?'

And the king will say to them in reply, 'Amen, I say to you, whatever you did for one of these least brothers of mine, you did for me.'

It was the second day of the conclave and the cardinals were getting ready to cast their fifth ballot to elect a new pope.

The Sistine Chapel grew very silent as each cardinal looked down at his ballot and prayerfully thought about which cardinal to nominate.

Cardinal Jorge Bergoglio from Argentina stared at his empty ballot and began to pray to the HolySpirit.

As he prayed, his eyes became very heavy. He tried to keep them open, but it became too difficult. Soon he fell into a deep sleep.

When Cardinal Jorge awoke, he found himself standing in the Piazza in Assisi. Looking around, he was surprised to see that it didn't look anything like it did several months ago when he was there on pilgrimage.

Something was very strange. Everyone was dressed in thirteenth-century attire. There must be some celebration, the cardinal thought to himself. I wonder if they are celebrating some special event. It couldn't be the Feast of St. Francis as this is March and the feast of St. Francis isn't until October.

"**I**s this some special celebration today?" the cardinal asked a group of young children as they walked by giggling.

"**O**h, but it is a very special day my beloved brother," a man's voice replied.

Cardinal Jorge turned around and was astonished at what he saw.

"St. Francis? No, It can't be you. You have been in heaven for almost eight hundred years. How could this be possible?"

"Well, you were praying to the Holy Spirit for guidance, so He sent you here so I could guide you."

"I don't understand." The cardinal shook his head in amazement. "I remember going to the Sistine Chapel this morning so we could vote for a new pope. We were getting ready to cast another ballot. I must have fallen asleep, and now I find myself in the middle of the Piazza here in Assisi."

"Isn't it lovely this time of year? Come, let's take a little walk." Francis took the cardinal by the arm and they began walking.

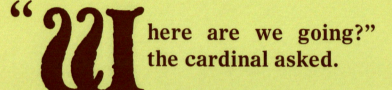

"Where are we going?" the cardinal asked.

"You will see. It is a very special place and one that you will surely recognize."

Francis and Cardinal Jorge walked down the hill from Assisi through fields of beautiful wildflowers until they found themselves in front of a small church.

"San Damiano," the cardinal said.

"Yes, this is where it all began. This is a very special place for me."

"I hear you had a hand in fixing it up," the cardinal said with a laugh.

Francis laughed too. "It was a labor of love."

"So, Francis, why am I here?"

"As I was praying here one day, I looked up at the crucifix that was hanging in the broken-down church and heard these words, 'Francis, rebuild my church. As you can see it has fallen into ruin.'"

"I know the story well," Cardinal Jorge said.

"So, seeing that the church needed a lot of work, I set out to fix it," Francis continued. "Stone by stone I worked on it until it was finished. It was only later that I understood what God really wanted me to do. What He asked me to do, I did. However, the work isn't finished. There is still more rebuilding of our church that must be done."

"There just aren't enough good workers in the vineyard to finish the work," the cardinal explained.

Francis placed his hand on the cardinal's shoulder. "Then you must find more workers," he said. "Dedicated workers, compassionate workers, who understand it is the heart not the head that will finish the rebuilding of our church."

"But I am only one person," Cardinal Jorge protested. "it will take more than myself to make this happen."

Francis turned around and pointed to the small church behind him. "My brother, see what one person can do when the will of our Father is behind us? My hands laid the stones, but it was the love I have for the One who asked me to do the work that made it all possible.

"You must find those sisters and brothers who—through their love of our Father—are willing to make the sacrifices to finish what was begun here."

"I understand," the cardinal replied. "I prayed for guidance and now I must decide who to cast my vote for. There are so many good men that can do what you are asking, it is difficult to choose just one. Can you give me some ideas?" he asked.

"**O**ur brother who is chosen must have an open and loving heart and must always *remember the poor*," Francis told Jorge. "He must see that the riches of the church are not in the treasures the church keeps locked up in vaults, or in fine clothes or fancy places to live."

Francis placed his hand on Cardinal Jorge's heart. "No, my brother, the riches of the church are here."

The saint looked him in the eyes and said once more, "The riches of the church are here."

Back in the Sistine Chapel Cardinal Jorge continued to look at the ballot in front of him. Then he smiled and wrote down the name of the man he felt could help St. Francis finish what he started so long ago.

he pushed his chair back from the table, walked to the altar, and placed his ballot in the chalice.

One by one the ballots were cast. Once the ballots were counted, the name of the cardinal who received two-thirds of the votes was announced, and he was asked if he would accept the nomination.

There was a moment of silence as Cardinal Jorge Bergoglio tried to understand what was just asked of him. The cardinal next to him whispered, *"Remember the poor."*

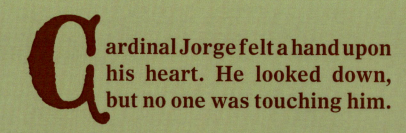

Cardinal Jorge felt a hand upon his heart. He looked down, but no one was touching him.

With an abundance of love for the church, Cardinal Jorge answered, "Yes, I will accept the papacy."

"What name have you chosen?"

"I choose Francis. I choose Francis."

Pope Francis then made his way out onto the balcony of St. Peter's Basilica. He greeted the crowd in a simple white vestment and asked them to pray for him. The crowd responded with shouts of approval for this poor man of Argentina, who—because of his love of the poor—chose the name of Francis, the poor man of Assisi.

To be continued...